Truly Foul & Cheesy™

Mummy Mania Facts & Jokes

This Truly Foul & Cheesy book belongs to:

....

Written by
John Townsend

Illustrated by
David Antram

BOOK HOUSE
a SALARIYA imprint

Introduction

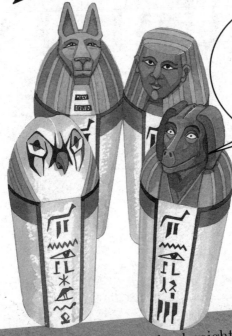

This book is like a mummy's coffin - packed with revolting bits.

Warning – reading this book might not make you **LOL** (laugh out loud) but it could make you **GOL** (groan out loud), feel sick out loud or **SEL** (scream even louder). If you are reading this in a library by a **SILENCE** sign… get ready to be thrown out!

Truly Foul & Cheesy™
Mummy Mania
Facts
& Jokes

Published in Great Britain in MMXVIII by
Book House, an imprint of
The Salariya Book Company Ltd
25 Marlborough Place, Brighton BN1 1UB
www.salariya.com

ISBN: 978-1-912233-01-4

SALARIYA

1 3 5 7 9 8 6 4 2

A CIP catalogue record for this book is available
from the British Library.

Printed and bound in China.
Printed on paper from sustainable sources.

Created and designed by
David Salariya.

Visit
www.salariya.com
for our online catalogue and
free fun stuff.

PAPER FROM

SUSTAINABLE
FORESTS

Author:
John Townsend worked as a
secondary school teacher before
becoming a full-time writer.
He specialises in illuminating and
humorous information books for
all ages.

Artist:
David Antram studied at
Eastbourne College of Art and then
worked in advertising for 15 years
before becoming a full-time artist.
He has illustrated many children's
non-fiction books.

Disclaimer: The author really hasn't made anything up in this book (apart from some daft limericks and jokes). He checked out the foul facts as best he could and even double-checked the fouler bits to make sure – so please don't get too upset if you find out something different or meet an Egyptologist, an archaeologist or any other 'ologist' who happens to know better. And if a mummy tells you anything at all… RUN!

'If I had my way, I'd RATIFY the lot!'

Official Warning

This book contains nuts – or at least lots of nutty stuff about real mummies in real museums. The weird, wacky, yucky world of mummification and the hundreds of places that store or display mummies can reveal fascinating, strange and even disgusting secrets.

There are certainly spooky stories about preserved bodies from ancient cultures, and the latest scientific techniques can now reveal even more. Mummies from around the world are about to tell us about human lives thousands of years ago. Get ready for plenty of amazing, scary, foul and revoltingly cheesy facts with jokes. Be prepared to be unprepared...

Mummy Limerick

When mummies lie in
a museum,
Huge crowds will queue up
just to see 'em
And stare in a daze
At the pickled displays...
How we love 'em – but who'd
want to be 'em?

3 Mummy Riddles

Q: During which age did
   the mummies first live?
A: The band-age

Q: What is a mummy's
   favourite kind of coffee?
A: De-coffin-ated

Q: What did the sign in the
   Egyptian museum say?
A: 'Satisfaction guaranteed or
   your mummy back.'

Keep It Under Wraps

In many a museum cellar
Lurks a mummified
Cobwebby dweller,
As if in its tomb,
But now in the gloom...
It stirs.... Eeek! (No wonder
this book's a best-seller!)

Beware of museums where
mummies are kept.
No one who stayed overnight
ever slept
Where mummified bodies lie lit
by moonlight...
Waiting to stir in the cold
DEAD of night.

One Day in the Mummy Museum...

'And this mummy over here,' croaked the 90-year-old museum guide, 'is five thousand, sixty-nine and a half years old. On its left, you can see another mummy which is four thousand and sixty-nine years old, six months.'

'Wow! That's amazing,' said a little lad in the audience, 'how can you age it so accurately to the exact month?'

'Well that's simple,' answered the old fellow, 'One was five thousand years old and the other was four thousand years old when I started working here 69½ years ago.'

The Rotten Facts

Look away now if you don't like basic biology and smelly science. It's all about life, death and rotters. Yes, dead bodies rot because of all the micro-organisms (like bacteria) that chomp away on skin and flesh, or nibble away from the inside on all those gooey organs. Under 'normal' conditions, a dead body will start to decompose in just a few days and after only months, little more than bones remain. But sometimes a dead body won't decay at all. If no air, moisture and micro-organisms can get to work on a corpse, it can last indefinitely.

Help - I'm being pickled!

What is a Mummy?

Any dead body (human or animal, from anywhere in the world) that hasn't rotted is a mummy. To be mummified, a body is simply preserved, either deliberately or by accident. Either someone made the mummy (so it's artificial) or something (such as unusual conditions) produced the mummy naturally. In both cases, the dead body does not decay and become a skeleton, as the skin (or fur) and flesh are preserved.

You name it, we'll mummify it.

Artificial mummies were made deliberately by people in various civilisations (such as ancient Egypt); often using different methods to prevent decay.

Accidental (or natural) mummies were (and still are) created accidentally by nature – through drying, freezing, or other natural processes. Some accidental mummies can be very old.

Where Does the Word 'Mummy' Come From?

'Mummy' comes from the Arabic word 'mumia' which means pitch or wax (bitumen). Originally, people believed pitch or wax was the stuff responsible for the lasting mummification effects.

DID YOU KNOW?

All kinds of animals can be mummies. At the Smithsonian Museum in Washington, you can see bull mummies and mummies of cats, ibises (sacred Egyptian wading birds), hawks, crocodiles, dogs, and even a baboon.

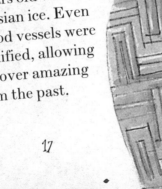

Other animals have been mummified naturally in bogs, pits or frozen soil. In 2010, a mummified woolly mammoth nearly 40,000 years old was found in the Russian ice. Even its brain and blood vessels were perfectly mummified, allowing scientists to discover amazing information from the past.

Why All the Fuss?

When archaeologists first began finding ancient human mummies, often buried with treasures, there was great excitement.

I'm not too sure about my birthday present, dear.

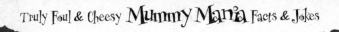

There were many mysteries to solve, but also money to be made, as many rich people wanted to own not just the treasures, but also the mummies as well. One hundred and fifty years ago, there was money to be made in digging up mummies and selling them around the world. Mummies became big business.

Once it's unwrapped, it will look stunning in the conservatory.

Two archaeologists are excavating a tomb in Egypt...

Arch 1: I just found another tomb of a mummified pharaoh.

Arch 2: Are you serious?

Arch 1: No bones about it!

Arch 2: It looks like the mummy is covered in chocolate and nuts.

Arch 1: In that case, it must be Pharaoh Rocher.

Arch 2: Do you like working with mummies?

Arch 1: Of corpse.

Arch 2: So why are you crying as you sift through the rubble of this pyramid?

Arch 1: Because my work is in ruins. It's a
dead-end job.

Arch 2: Doh!

Mummies On The Move

For over 200 years people have flocked to see mummies in museums. Such macabre ancient remains weren't just seen as spooky, but also fascinating and mysteriously exotic. Imagine being able to stand beside preserved bodies that have lasted for centuries, even millennia, giving a rare glimpse of our ancestors.

It is only more recently that we have begun asking questions about the plundering of ancient tombs and of displaying dead people from long ago. Is it right to display 'gruesome relics' in museums for the public to gawp at? Today, some mummies have been hidden away and are now kept out of sight. What do you think about that?

Don't Lose Mummy

Shock horror – many mummies are vanishing! Some mummies are disappearing because they haven't been kept very well in museums over the years. Bright lights, damp or even insect damage have made some mummies crumble to dust.

Other mummies are disappearing from public view due to complaints that they're either too gross or need more respect. Even ancient mummies (including those from Egypt) are being removed from some museums, especially in the United States and Europe. Yet many archaeologists and other scientists still believe museum mummies provide important education about lost civilisations – as well as teaching about death itself.

At least this stops me getting sunburn.

Ancient Egyptians

This recipe says use hot oils.

It'll get mummified!

Darling, I think I'm going to be a mummy.

The most famous mummies we know about today were kings in Egypt from 3000 to 5000 years ago (called pharaohs). The people believed a pharaoh was a living god who had to be kept happy in life and remembered long after death. The Egyptians believed in an afterlife so it was important to preserve each pharaoh in the best condition for the next life. This was done by drying out the body and wrapping it tightly in linen bandages, to stop the rot setting in. This process is called mummification.

The Egyptians believed dead leaders and their families had to be mummified by an expert team of mummy-makers. Here's their recipe:

1 Take one dead pharaoh and give it a good scrub.

2 Remove all the organs, apart from the heart.

3 Poke a long hook up the nose and mash the brain. Pull out goo through nostrils.

4 After 40 days stuff with cloth and sawdust.

5 Cover body in oils and wrap with long cloth strip

6 Place in stone coffin called a sarcophagus, seal tightly and leave to stand forever.

7 Lie back and imagine a perfect afterlife... being admired in a cosy museum.

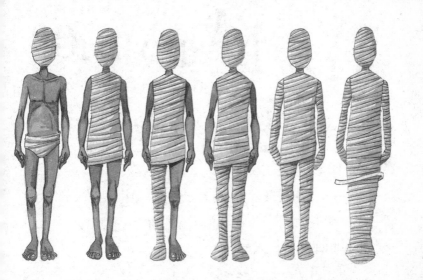

DID YOU KNOW?

Unwrapped, the bandages of an ancient Egyptian mummy could stretch for 1.6 km. That's miles better than just a few strips (actually, that's pretty much one whole mile of bandage).

The Mummies Return

Because so many Egyptian mummies and treasures were stolen from pyramids and tombs, it's hardly surprising that Egypt would like them returned. In 2009, 'Operation Mummy's Curse' began to fight the trade in ancient objects, and particularly the smuggling of Egyptian artefacts into the United States.

In Fact...
(brace yourself for a 'gross alert')

A 3,000-year-old stolen mummy hand was found at a studio, being used as a prop for actors to wave around – **YUCK!** You've got to hand it to the USA folks (groan) – they sent it back to Egypt, along with a mummy's shroud and painted coffins. The Grand Egyptian Museum in Cairo was pleased to welcome them home. **CHEESY ALERT...** Maybe they had to get a Cairo-practor to fit together all the body parts!

(Yes, that was a rubbish joke as a real chiropractor treats pains by pressing a person's joints and doesn't normally work on dead mummies – only live ones).

33

British Mummies

Many museums in Britain are chock-a-block with mummies and ancient Egyptian objects. You might be surprised at what's on display or tucked away in basements. The British Museum in London has the biggest collection in three rooms:

1 The museum has over 120 human mummies in its collection.

2 As well as humans, over 300 animal mummies are stored in the museum.

This dead croc's got a frog in its throat. It's a croak-a-dile.

3 The longest animal mummy is a 4-metre-long crocodile.

4 Over 80 mummies in the museum collection are from Egypt.

5 Just over 40 mummies are from Sudan.

Can You Believe It?

The first mummies to enter the British Museum were fakes. The first genuine mummies were acquired in 1756. Most of the mummies still have their wrappings in place. No mummy has been unwrapped at the museum since the 1790s. You may have seen some if you saw *Night at the Museum: Secret of the Tomb*, which was filmed in the British Museum. Would you dare spend the night alone among all those mummies?

I might cry as I'm a bit of a mummy's boy.

A Juicy Piece of Gossip from the British Museum...

One of the British Museum's mummies is nicknamed 'Ginger' because of its unusual hair colour. It actually dates from before the time Egyptians began mummifying their dead regularly. Ginger was an adult male who died more than 5,000 years ago and was buried in direct contact with the dry desert sand, which is why the body didn't decay. Other early Egyptian mummies were also created naturally this way, but he is thought to be the oldest.

Like many mummies, Ginger had a creepy tale to tell. It was said that when the Museum was looking for a mummy in the 19th century, this specimen was bought from a dodgy dealer, who apparently had a relative of similar size and appearance to the mummy (also with ginger hair), who strangely disappeared at the time the mummy was bought...

However, experts at the British Museum have proved Ginger was genuine and probably a murder victim, as a scan showed an injury to his shoulder blade and a shattered rib underneath, suggesting a stab wound killed him.

Visitors to the museum can now use a touch screen on a virtual operating table to examine the body and find clues about Ginger's life and death. Why not pop along and meet him?

Ginger was the first baker ever. He invented gingerbread.

Liverpool Mummies

Liverpool's World Museum has over 16,000 objects from ancient Egypt, including the mummy of a young boy. Visitors are invited to explore the special Mummy Room, to read spells from the Book of the Dead and even sniff ingredients used in mummification. (No, it's not SPHYNX Body Spray). But there's also a whiff of cat lingering in Liverpool. Yes, cat mummies have been seen (and probably smelt) in the city.

When the museum's 'Animal Mummies Revealed' exhibition closed in 2017, over 100,000 people had seen the 60 or so specimens – mummified jackals, crocodiles, birds and, yes, cats. Cat mummies had a grisly history in Liverpool.

It looks like the cat's eaten the budgie.

In 1890, about 180,000 unwrapped mummified cats arrived from Egypt at the city's docks, where they were sold at auction. At that time, these mummies weren't seen as valuable objects and had just been used as ballast to balance the ship during the voyage. So who bought them all? Mainly farmers – to crush them all up and spread on fields like manure. If that wasn't bad enough, the auctioneer even used a cat's head as a hammer to strike the sale. How foul is that? But worse was to come…

Night at the Meowseum

A few cat mummies did get rescued and sent to Liverpool's museum, but they all met their fate in World War 2. In the blitz of 1941, the cat mummies and more than 3,000 Egyptian objects were destroyed when the museum was hit by a bomb. Maybe it was a mummy's curse at work…

REVENGE of the Mummy Cat?

Did you hear about the cat that went into the museum to have her kittens behind a sarcophagus? She was instantly mummified.

When the kittens' father came to visit, he was instantly daddified. Tee hee.

I sphinx these puns are so a-mews-ing...

Talking of Cats...

Where did all those mummified cats come from?

In 1888 an Egyptian farmer digging in the desert a hundred miles from Cairo struck a 'seam of cats' when he apparently fell into a hole. This was a tunnel packed with hundreds of thousands of ancient mummified cats. News soon spread and locals came in search of gold. They found a life-size bronze sarcophagus with a cat inside but apart from that, there were just cats upon cats upon cats. They'd been bred in large numbers just to be killed, wrapped in bandages and used as lucky charms to gain favours with the gods.

GROSS ALERT...

People dug out all the cat mummies and peeled the wrappings off each one, then stripped off the brittle fur, and piled the bones in black heaps. The rags and other crumbly bits were carted off in donkey loads to be spread on the fields as fertiliser. CATastrophic, or what?

Meanwhile, Back at the Museums...

Just imagine coming face to face with somebody (yes, some body) who is thousands of years old. You can do just that, as well as admire some of their amazing possessions, in lots of British museums.

The National Museum of Scotland in Edinburgh has an impressive collection, discovered in Egyptian tombs long ago. Just who was the young woman and child buried with magnificent gold and luxurious finery in about 1550 BC? The stunning gold painted coffin suggests the woman may have been a queen. Now known as 'The Qurna Queen', she wore a magnificent collar of gold rings, a pair of gold earrings, two pairs of gold bracelets and a girdle of rings (over 90% pure gold). Buried with her, to stop her getting hungry in the afterlife, was bread and fruit; grapes, dates and a pomegranate. Alas, these are now a tad past their sell-by date.

You can even see what this tall, elegant woman looked like. Experts have scanned her skull to help them make a realistic model of her face. You can easily go online, take a peek and say hi!

In Swansea, South Wales, you can not only see a mummy on display in the museum, but also visit the Egypt Centre with all sorts of bits and pieces from ancient Egyptian life – even ancient earplugs made of metal discs with grooved edges worn in a hole in the earlobe (as jewellery, rather than plugs to keep out the noise from all those pyramid builders).

In Northern Ireland, the Ulster Museum has a great Egyptian collection, including the mummy of an Egyptian aristocrat, Lady Takabuti. Her head is unwrapped so you can see her face up-close and actually meet someone who's 2700 years old.

Honey, what's your mother doing here?

EEK
– It Must Be a Mummy's Curse!

Manchester Museum and its amazing Egyptian collection made world news in 2013 when something creepy happened not just in the dead of night… but in broad daylight. It wasn't anything to do with Asru, the mummy and her coffin nearby, or a couple of mummies from the Roman period. No, this was a little Egyptian statue which began to spin ALL BY ITSELF. It mysteriously started moving very slowly and even scientists were stumped – was it haunted? Yikes!

One good turn deserves another...

The statue rotated 180 degrees every three days... without anyone touching it, as it was locked inside a glass case. The museum's curator kept turning it back, knowing the ancient Egyptians believed if the mummy was destroyed then the statuette buried alongside it was meant to take on its spirit. A time lapse video was sped up to show the statue was really moving without being touched. Was the mummy's spirit trying to say something?

Scientists blame vibrations from footsteps around the room for causing the movement... but why didn't other exhibits do the same? Apparently, the statue isn't quite flat underneath and has a little bump on its bottom. That's enough to make anyone have a funny turn!

There again... maybe mummies in museums dance about at night and have a bit of a party.

Limerick Time

This mummy is really a chap
Who long ago had a mishap
And then got preserved
(No doubt well-deserved)
While dancing to music – cool
WRAP! (Or just old ragtime.)

Not Funny, Mummy

It isn't much fun as
a mummy,
You could say it's
really a bind,
With my bandages
yucky and gummy...
How I long to relax
and unwind.

Museums of Egypt

As you would expect, the most famous (and sometimes scariest) Egyptian mummies can be seen in the city museums of Egypt, such as in Cairo and Luxor.

King Ramses the Second (also known as Ramesses the Great) became the ruler of Egypt in his early twenties (around 1279 BC) and ruled for 66 years until his death (1213 BC) – when he was over ninety years old.

I'm Ramses as a young man...

And I'm Ramses as an old man!

Today, the mummy of this great pharaoh is one of the best-preserved mummies in the world and rests in the Cairo Museum in Egypt. It shows that he stood over six feet tall (almost 2 metres), with a strong, jutting jaw, thin nose, thick lips and red hair. He suffered from dental problems, severe arthritis and hardening of the arteries, and most probably died from old age or heart failure (not surprising in his mid-nineties and with 200 wives!)

The linen over Ramses II's body is covered in hieroglyphics, which explain that, after he was first buried in the Valley of the Kings, priests were forced to move the mummy because of looting.

FOUL
ALERT...

About a hundred years after his mummy was discovered, archaeologists noticed the mummy was getting a bit mouldy – with a yucky fungal infection. So it was off to the doctors. Yes, the mummy (at the age of around 3,300 years in 1976) was flown to Paris. Weirdly, the great pharaoh had to be given an Egyptian passport, in which his occupation was listed as 'King (deceased)'. You'll be pleased to know the treatment did the trick and he could be returned to Cairo a lot healthier – and less smelly.

AAAAAH!
The Screaming Mummy

Also in Cairo Museum is a particularly scary-looking mummy that was found in the same set of tombs as Ramesses the Great in 1886. Brace yourself… It was a blood-curdling discovery. The mummy was of a young man with his hands and feet bound, and his face contorted in an everlasting scream of pain.

This body, unlike all other mummies, was inside a plain, undecorated coffin that offered no clues to who he was. Not only that, all his organs were intact, which is not the usual way with Egyptian mummification. He wasn't bandaged in linen but rolled up in sheepskin. It's thought he could have been poisoned as a punishment and buried alive, as he screamed in agony. Don't have nightmares!

AAAHHHHHHAAAAVVVV

Tutankhamun

Probably the most famous of all the Egyptian kings is King Tut, better known as Tutankhamun. That's because of his stunning golden death mask, stories of his mummy's curse and because the treasures from his tomb have toured the world, with many millions of people getting to see the possessions of the boy king. 'Tutanmania' has swept the world.

In 1922 Howard Carter, a British archaeologist, discovered a tomb in The Valley of the Kings. Hidden inside was the mummy of Tutankhamun, surrounded by treasures. Tutankhamun died in about 1324 BC aged around 19, after reigning for nine years. His magnificent solid gold funeral mask is encrusted with lapis lazuli and semi-precious stones. The restored mask is on display at the Egyptian Museum in Cairo.

In 2007, 85 years to the day since it was discovered, Tutankhamun's mummy went on display for the first time in his underground tomb at Luxor. Although all the treasures from the tomb have been removed, the mummy itself had been kept in its sarcophagus in the burial chamber. The boy king was finally brought out of hiding and put on public display for all to see. His linen-wrapped mummy is displayed in a special climate-controlled glass box.

I wonder if he knows about the mummy's curse.

What Happened to King Tut?

Historians have never been sure how or
why Tutankhamun died so young. Some
said a hole in the mummy's skull showed
he had been murdered. He also had broken
bones. Other experts thought he might have
been killed by a hippopotamus, as Ancient
Egyptians hunted hippos for sport. Statues
found in the tomb show him throwing a
harpoon, so maybe he was killed in a hunting
accident. There again, he may have been
killed by a chariot crashing into him. It's
hard to be sure because he wasn't mummified
properly, as the body cooked and burned due
to all the oils used on him. His flesh stuck to
the inside of the coffin, so getting him out
caused a bit of a mess.

There were many mysteries and myths about Tutankhamun in both life and death. Lord Carnarvon, who paid for the excavation in 1922, died suddenly soon afterwards. As he died, the lights in Cairo failed and his dog back home howled. Superstitious people said a curse was at work. Then, in 1944, a tomb robber reached into another coffin to steal some gold. The lid fell and trapped him, before the roof fell in and killed him. They know when he died because they found that day's newspaper in his skeleton's tattered coat. Was this the mummy's revenge?

Did You Know?

Treasures from Tutankhamun's tomb have travelled across the world. An exhibition in The British Museum in 1972 was attended by 1.6 million visitors, making it the most popular exhibition in the museum's history. The 1977–79 exhibition in the US was attended by over 8 million people. The most popular object from the tomb was the golden death mask topped by a cobra and vulture.

Today you can see (and smell) something of Tutankhamun in Dorchester, England. An exhibition recreated the treasures using mainly the same materials and methods, making them as close as possible to the originals now in Egypt. A reconstruction of the tomb itself has a whiff of history about it, as the creators have recreated the smells that Carter described on finding the tomb. You could say it's more like a 'phew-seum'.

What's King Tut's favourite food?

King Tut-key fried chicken.

Silly riddle

Q: How do you open the door at the Cairo Museum?

A: Toot-and-come-in!

Mummies and Curses

During the 19th century, following the discovery of the first tombs in Egypt, there was huge interest across Europe in Egyptology. Victorian Britain couldn't get enough of mummy-mania. Wealthy people would even hold mummy parties to impress their friends. Oh yes, they would buy a real mummy, invite their guests, lower the lights and unwrap the mummy in front of everyone. No doubt there were squeals of horror or even delight – but sadly, such parties destroyed hundreds of mummies forever. Exposing the ancient remains to the air caused them to fall apart.

Even more terrible were stage shows held in London theatres, where the tension was built up with gruesome tales of 'the pharaoh's curse' just as a mummy was dramatically unwrapped in front of gasping audiences. The horror of these tasteless public 'undressings', with little respect for the dead, probably inspired scary stories of mummy revenge. Years later, horror movies kept up the idea of mummies striking back, and now mummy costumes at Halloween are supposed to scare us along with zombies and ghosts.

Ladies and gentlemen, this gold charm was meant to protect the mummy from nincompoops like us.

The British Museum's Cursed Mummy

BEWARE - this is such a chilling tale, you really shouldn't read it after dark...

There again, it's mainly a load of rubbish (possibly!)

70

In one of the British Museum's Egypt Rooms, you can see item 22542 – if you dare. Those who cast their eyes on this object may never be the same again, or so the story goes. You will be staring into the eyes of an ancient face – not a mummy, but a beautifully painted coffin lid that's 3,000 years old. The mummy herself is missing and no one knows where she is or who she was – maybe a priestess of the Temple of Amen-Ra? And maybe – just maybe – she placed a curse on what became called The Unlucky Mummy, which is, in fact, 'the painted wooden mummy-board of an unidentified woman' acquired by the British Museum in 1889.

From the time that mummy case was first discovered, strange deaths followed its journey to the British Museum. Sudden death has haunted those who've handled this ancient relic ever since (according to the scary myth).

The Myth of 'The Unlucky' Mummy

Happy Mummy's Day!

After the luxury liner, the Titanic, sank in 1912, an unlucky mummy's curse was whispered to be responsible for the disaster. The myth goes like this:

In the late 1890's a rich Englishman visiting the archaeological digs in Egypt bought the coffin and mummy of The Princess of Amen-Ra. He arranged for it to be shipped back to his home, but was not there to receive it. He disappeared, never to be found. One of his friends on the trip later died, another lost an arm in an accident and a third lost all of his money.

The coffin reached England, where a businessman bought it. Immediately, three members of his family were injured in a car crash and his house caught fire. Convinced that the mummy was unlucky, the man donated it to the British Museum.

The staff at the museum reported hearing loud banging and crying noises coming from the coffin at night. Things were thrown around the exhibit room without explanation. After a guide in the room died suddenly, a photographer took a photo of the coffin. When he developed it, the image that appeared was so horrifying that the photographer leapt from a window.

The museum now wanted to get rid of the unlucky mummy, so it was sold to an American archaeologist, who sent it to the United States on board the Titanic. And you know what happened next...

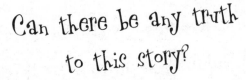

Can there be any truth to this story?

Shipping records show no mummy was on board the Titanic. No survivor ever mentioned sharing a lifeboat with a mummy or coffin! Apart from that, 'The Unlucky Mummy' hadn't left the British Museum since 1889. But maybe this myth had a grain of truth…

Long ago, two Englishmen claimed they knew someone who bought a mummy in Egypt and placed it in his home. The next morning every breakable item in the room had been smashed. The next night the mummy was left in another room and the same happened.

When the men saw the coffin lid of Priestess Amun in the British Museum, they thought the face on it was so scary that they linked it to their friend's weird experience. They sold the tale to the newspapers and it grew to include the Titanic myth. Maybe the link to a ship was based on the loss of an Egyptian sarcophagus in 1838. It was being shipped to the British Museum when the ship carrying it, the Beatrice, sank in deep water. That sarcophagus of the pharaoh Menkaura remains one of history's vanished treasures, and has never been found at the bottom of the sea.

Mummies on the Market

For wealthy American and European tourists in the 19th century, Egypt was the place to visit. Bringing home a mummy as a souvenir to keep in the living room or even the bedroom was seen as very stylish. Mummy hands, feet and heads were frequently displayed around the house, often on the mantelpiece. One Chicago store apparently displayed a mummy said to be 'Pharaoh's daughter who discovered Moses in the bulrushes'.

Mummies also had other uses, particularly when they were chopped up... FOUL ALERT!

Mashed-up Mummies

Can you believe that anyone would sprinkle powdered mummy into hot water and drink it? Some people were convinced this medicine would cure all kinds of ailments. A quick swig of mummy broth was thought to do you the world of good (please don't try this next time you have a cold, as it could give you a sore-cough-or-gas).

Can someone give me a hand?

Mummy Brown

For many years, ground-up ancient Egyptian human and cat mummies appeared in pictures – as paint. Artists liked a particular shade of yucky brown in their masterpieces, so paint makers mixed in powdered mummies and called the paint **Mummy Brown**. It certainly added a lot of body into their art.

This shade of brown is DEAD right.

Mummies in China

Ancient mummies have been found in tombs in China and they can reveal all kinds of secrets. A 3,600-year-old mummy of a woman shows she'd received brain surgery – or at least a hole drilled into her skull, which had begun to heal.

Another mummy was the wife of a Chinese ruler and known as Lady Dai, who died about 2,200 years ago. Scans showed she died from a heart-attack at 50 years of age due to obesity. When her mummy was examined, she still had moist skin, her joints were still flexible and even her eyelashes and the hair in her nostrils remained. Lady Dai was found in an airtight tomb 12 metres (40 feet) underground, locked inside four layers of coffins. Her body had been buried in 20 layers of silk.

Mummies in South America

It's a bit Chile in here.

2,000 years before the Egyptians started mummification, the Chinchorro people, who lived on the coast of the Atacama Desert in South America (Peru and Chile today) were already mummifying their dead people. The oldest Chinchorro mummies date back about 7,000 years. The dead bodies had their organs removed, their skin was sewed back and their bodies were painted black from head to toe. Then the Chinchorro people would place wigs on the heads, and they left the eyes and mouths open. Some even had tattoos. Unfortunately, some on display in Arica Museum in Chile are going black, slimy, oozy and squidgy. After all, you can't expect anyone to be at their best at 7,000 years old.

Bog Mummies

If you happen to visit the National Museum of Ireland in Dublin, you could meet a 'natural' mummy, known as a 'bog man' or Cashel Man. In 2011, a man's body was found in an Irish bog – he had been there for 4,000 years and was preserved in the peat. Archaeologists have been able to study the mummy to find out more about life in the Bronze Age. Usually archaeologists are fairly polite but they say Cashel Man is 'the oldest fleshed bog body in Europe'. How rude!

Ice Mummies

Hikers in the Alps of Austria came face to face with a frozen body in 1991. This 'ice mummy' was 5,300 years old and he's now known as Otzi. You can see him and his belongings at the South Tyrol Museum of Archaeology in Bolzano, Italy. But now there are more of him! His mummy has been scanned and 3D printed, to create three life-size Ötzi clones. The Iceman's first two 3D prints are on display at the DNA Learning Center in New York. The third life-size print is in a travelling exhibit, making Otzi quite a celebrity.

Mmm... I love an ice mummy!

Another famous frozen mummy is the Siberian Ice Maiden, better known as the Ukok Princess. This 2,500-year-old lady who died in her twenties is well-known for her stunning tattoos, which are said to be the most elaborate of their kind anywhere on Earth. But not everyone was happy about removing her from her icy tomb. Local people believe bad things have happened because her body has been disturbed. Forest fires, earthquakes and illnesses have been blamed on her curse. Yet scientists believe that they have gained amazing historical knowledge from her remains. Even so, the fear of an icy curse still looms for some of those who discovered the mummy.

Don't you think my tattoos are INK-credible?

In 1995, high in the Andes Mountains of Peru, a volcano melted the ice that had preserved 'the ice maiden', now called Juanita. She was about 12-14 years old when she died 500 years ago - probably killed as a sacrifice to please the Inca gods. If you'd like to say hello to Juanita, she and 13 similar mummies are rotated and displayed in a glass container at -20°C in the Arequipa Museum in Peru. You'd better wear a thick vest.

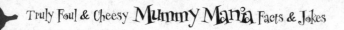

'Plaster Mummies' of Vesuvius

Look out - the volcano's exploding!

When the Italian volcano Vesuvius erupted in AD 79, the gas and ash that poured from the crater killed thousands of people in nearby Pompeii and Herculaneum. Everyone was going about their daily lives when they were preserved in an instant. Their bodies were buried in ash and preserved for hundreds of years. When archaeologists began digging into the ash, they found people-shaped holes that were once bodies of the victims. By pouring liquid plaster into these holes, scientists have been able to make detailed casts of the citizens of ancient Pompeii. Many visitors go to see these 'plaster mummies' at the Antiquarium Museum, which is just up the street from the Porta Marina entrance to Pompeii. You can see mummy-like statues of men, women, children and animals that lived nearly 2,000 years ago.

This will make a great statue for my garden.

Nightmare at the Mummy Museum

Just cut out the cheesy jokes.

It must be one of the most gruesome museums in the world – but thousands of visitors queue up each week to see the 'zombies' inside the Guanajuato Mummy Museum in Mexico. In fact, they are really mummies (not the visitors but the exhibits) – but not from ancient times at all.

Over one hundred bodies of mummified men, women and children are on display, many with gaping mouths – as if screaming. These bodies had been buried in sealed tombs nearby during a cholera outbreak in 1833. The Museum of the Mummies now displays these haunting figures, standing in rows for visitors to walk past and take selfies beside. Many would argue this is taking 'mummies in museums' just too far. What do you think?

Museums with a head start

Some mummies aren't really mummies. They're just preserved heads that have been shrunk. You can sometimes see these gruesome objects in museums which display how other cultures once lived.

The Pitt Rivers Museum in Oxford, UK is like a packed warehouse of all kinds of treasures – but be warned of what you might meet down one of the shadowy aisles. Yes, you could come head to head with a shrunken head.

The shrunken heads on display in the Pitt Rivers Museum are from the Upper Amazon region of South America. They were made by the Shuar and Achuar peoples, who still live in the dense jungle. Men from these tribes kept enemy heads to capture souls and keep their power for their own people. You'll be relieved to know these people no longer kill enemies, cut off their heads and shrink them. This stopped by the 1960s.

Honey, I've Shrunk My Head

This was how it was done (look away now)

1 Skin the head and throw away the skull and brain.

2 Soak the skin in hot water and then pour in hot sand.

 **3** Repeat the hot sand treatment several times over a period of months.

4 Mould the nose and cheeks after each treatment.

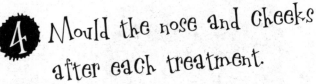 **5** Close the eyes and mouth and sew up with cotton string.

6 Blacken the face with vegetable dye to prevent the soul from escaping and seeking revenge on the killer.

7 String up the head on a cord and wear at ritual feasts.

I think I'm going to be sick.

European explorers collected shrunken heads as souvenirs. Those at the Pitt Rivers Museum were collected between 1871 and 1936. At that time, many fake heads were made from monkey or goat heads. FOUL ALERT... Some were even made from unclaimed human bodies in morgues and hospitals. Fortunately, times have changed for the better!

Today, much thought goes into museum exhibitions, especially when displaying human remains. The Pitt Rivers Museum often considers whether the way such objects are displayed is respectful, and tries to make the information 'appropriate and clearly communicated'.

Even so, whoever would want to spend a night alone in the room with the shrunken heads?

It would do your head in.

To do well at school, just visit the museum to get a head...

Mummified and Ratified

Rat 1: The Egyptians mummified a lot of rats, you know.

Rat 2: Are you sure?

Rat 1: Yes – many rat mummies had little coffins, too.

Don't get ratty with me.

Rat 2: Whatever for?

Rat 1: To keep them safe for the afterlife.
It was believed that rats ate the hearts
of sinners on judgment day.

Rat 2: Yuk!

Rat 1: And did you know that the pharaohs
were mummified with their hands
crossed over their chests?

Rat 2: I wonder why?

Rat 1: Maybe they thought there would be
lots of water slides in the afterlife. Tee hee!

I'm just worn out,
that's all. Life's a rat
race right now.

An Ancient Egyptian Version of TV's Masterchef

(Presenters Gregg & John, Narrator & Contestants Nef & Seti)

Gregg: Welcome to Master Mummy, where our contestants this week have the mother of all challenges...

John: Or rather the mummy of all challenges. They've got to prepare a real mummy. It could get messy – but it's no good going crying to mummy!

Gregg: Yes, they both have to make a mummy using similar ingredients. So who will we be sending home today?

John: It's a competition to prepare the best mummy in ancient Egypt. So welcome to the wabet.

Gregg: The rabbit?

John: No – the wabet. It's where Egyptian bodies get prepared to become mummies. Let's meet the contestants...

Nef: Hello, I'm Nef. I'm very nervous but I think I can do this even though I'm squeamish.

Gregg: Well good luck, Nef. I hope you can meet today's challenge. Who will you be mummifying for us today?

Nef: My mother-in-law – or as I now call her: Mummy-in-law.

John: So let's meet contestant number two.

Seti: Hello, I'm Seti. I've never made a mummy before but I've bandaged up my granny a few times so it should be a doddle.

Gregg: Do you think you've got what it takes?

Seti: Definitely. I've just got a dead pharaoh delivered. He's still quite fresh and I'm raring to go.

John: Don't forget to use a wooden tag to label your mummies. We don't want any mummy mix-ups when we pop them in the pyramid tomb in a sarcophagus.

Gregg: So it just remains for us to start the clock. Both contestants are now at their slabs, each with a body stretched in front of them, with a range of the best ingredients and natron salt for making a master mummy. The bodies have already had a good soak in natron solution for over a month.

John: You have just thirty minutes to mummify.
          May the best mummy win. GO!

Narrator: Nef is making a cheap 'basic range'
          mummy, using a cedar oil infusion, with a
          natron dressing and a light perfume
          drizzle.

Nef: (Dabbing perfume on herself) Silly to
          waste this on mother-in-law now.

It's best to take all this nonsense with a pinch of salt.

Narrator: Seti is preparing a mid-range mummy for only a mid-range pharaoh. The body has just been delivered from the 'ibu' tent of purification and the organs are about to be removed for pickling. Seti will be serving the mummy in a linen wrap and a spicy frankincense syrup on a bed of papyrus leaves.

Seti: (*Squeezing out a wet rag*) Firstly a quick wash with a solution of natron dissolved in water. (*Washes own arms while consulting a recipe book covered in hieroglyphics*) Oops, wrong body!

Gregg: Tell me what you're doing, Nef.

Nef: I'm using a slicer to cut open the body so that the organs can be removed for drying out. I'll need to use this clothes peg, too.

Gregg: For hanging up the organs to dry?

Nef: No, to put on my nose. It's a smelly job.
           I'm just taking out the liver, lungs,
           stomach and intestines. Phew!

Gregg: That's very brave of you.

Nef: Yes, I've got a lot of guts. With this gross
           recipe, you can easily get upset.

Gregg: So you've got to be heartless?

Nef: Certainly not – I've kept the heart inside.
           It will be needed in the afterlife.

John: Tell us what you're doing with all the other
           organs, Nef.

It's not the cough that carries you off...

It's the coffin they carry you off in.

Nef: I've popped them in canopic jars with images of the gods.

Narrator: Nef is washing out the body's inside with palm wine, then soaking it in more natron to dry out.

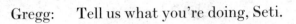

Gregg: Tell us what you're doing, Seti.

Seti: I'm making a very fine brain mash with this special tool I call a nose-pick. I just pop it up the pharaoh's nose like this... And when it reaches the brain, I just give it a little P.S.M.S.

John: Professional Skill and Medical Science?

Seti: No – Push, Squeeze, Mince and Squelch. The brain shoots out down the nose in one gooey mess. Are you all right?

John: I think I'm going to be sick... (*runs off*)

Gregg: Hurry, you need to be wrapping your bodies in bandages by now. Normally this should need twenty layers of linen over fifteen days.

Narrator: Nef is tucking little amulets into the bandages.

Nef: This is a scarab amulet, which is a lucky charm. It's for stopping my mummy's secrets getting found out.

John: You both have ten seconds left to complete your mummy...

Narrator: Nef is still tangled up in bandages.

Nef: I think I've finished. It's a wrap!

Gregg: Five seconds left.

Narrator: Seti has forgotten to put the heart back in, which is very important for the pharaoh in the afterlife.

John: One second...

Gregg: Stop! Stand back from your mummies.

John: Nef, I like your style. Neat bandaging here, just a few frayed edges but most parts sealed and wrapped.

Gregg: Seti, a mad panic to get the heart back in there but you just about did it.

John: To me, you've overdone the resin. The oils are coming over too strong. You don't want a Tutankhamun to happen, do you?

Nef: What's that?

John: He got mummy-fried. The embalming oils in Tutankhamun's mummy caught fire inside the sarcophagus and he cooked. Barbecued mummy isn't nice.

Narrator: So, who goes on to the next round? Which mummy will be going home on the bus? The judges are about to make their decision.

Gregg: One of you will be going through to the next round. One of you is about to be sent home. (*Scary music*)

John: The one of you going home is... (*VERY long pause*)

Gregg: Did I just hear you swear, Nef?

Nef: It wasn't me, honest.

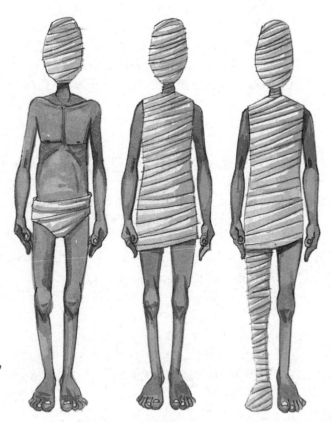

Gregg: Yikes – in that case… It's 'The Mummy's
      Curse'!

*(Sudden scary laugh. Both mummies sit up and
do triumphant high-fives as sinister music plays
and everyone runs off, screaming.)*

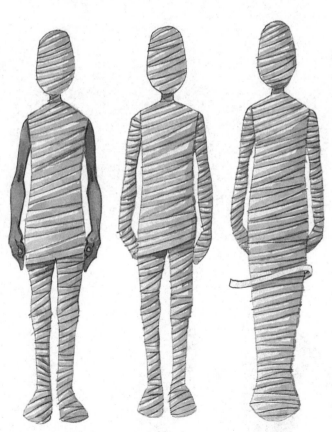

Egyptian Mummy (on phone):
Hello, I'd like to reserve a table for
the pharaoh Sakhrakhotep.

Restaurant:
Could you spell that, please?

Egyptian Mummy:
Of course. Bird, two triangles,
wavy line, the sun, bird again,
jackal's head and a scarab.

If you survived some of the truly foul facts and cheesy jokes in this book, take a look at the other wacky titles in this revolting series. They're all guaranteed to make you groan and squirm like never before. Share them with your friends AT YOUR OWN RISK!

QUIZ

1. How far could the unwrapped bandages of an Egyptian mummy stretch?

a) 1.6 km (1 mile)

b) 20 km (12.5 miles)

c) 2.5 km (1.5 miles)

2. What is the Siberian ice maiden mummy called?

a) Sleeping Beauty

b) Ukok Princess

c) Frostina

3. What was the name of the operation to prevent the trade in smuggled Egyptian artefacts?

a) Operation Mummy's Curse

b) Operation Ramesses' Revenge

c) Operation Sarcophagus Stakeout

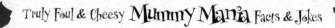

4. Which museum in Oxford, UK has shrunken heads in its collection?

a) Ashmolean Museum

b) Pitt Rivers Museum

c) Oxford Museum of Natural History

5. What is the name of the scary-looking mummy of a young man in Cairo Museum?

a) The Moaning Mummy

b) The Screaming Mummy

c) The Wailing Mummy

6. What did Howard Carter discover in 1922?

a) A new element in the periodic table

b) Cleopatra's wig

c) The tomb of Tutankhamun

7. What was Cashel Man's body naturally preserved in?

a) A bog

b) Quicksand

c) Vinegar

8. What colour hair did Ramses the Second have?

a) Red

b) Blue

c) Brown

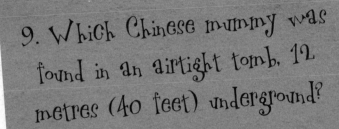

9. Which Chinese mummy was found in an airtight tomb, 12 metres (40 feet) underground?

a) Lady Lin

b) Lady Lulu

c) Lady Dai

10. What is the name of the people who lived in the Atacama desert and painted their mummies' bodies black?

a) Chinchorro

b) Chinchin

c) Cheesy

Answers:

1 = a
2 = b
3 = a
4 = b
5 = b
6 = c
7 = a
8 = a
9 = c
10 = a

GLOSSARY

Archaeologist: a person who studies excavated sites and artefacts to find out about past civilisations.

Bacteria: microscopic lifeforms, which are usually single-celled and often cause disease.

Cairo: a 1000-year-old Egyptian city, and the capital of modern-day Egypt.

Egyptologist: an archaeologist who specialises in studying the artefacts and ruins of Ancient Egypt.

Fertiliser: a substance, rich in nutrients, added to soil to make it more fertile and capable of growing crops.

Hieroglyphics: the Egyptian writing system, with an alphabet of stylised pictures or symbols.

The Blitz: the nighttime bombing raids carried out by Germany against London and other cities in Britain during the Second World War.

Valley of the Kings: the burial site of many pharaohs of Ancient Egypt, located to the west of the River Nile in Upper Egypt.

INDEX

Look out for other wacky books in this series... if you dare!

I finished reading this Truly Foul & Cheesy book on:

........../........../..........